'OURS IS A TRUE CHURCH OF GOD': WILLIAM PERKINS AND THE REFORMED DOCTRINE OF THE CHURCH

DONALD JOHN MACLEAN

The Latimer Trust

ISBN 978-1-906327-55-2

Cover photo: 'Close-up of beautiful stained glass transparent window from old church' by JoeyCheung

Published by the Latimer Trust March 2019.

The Latimer Trust (formerly Latimer House, Oxford) is a conservative Evangelical research organisation within the Church of England, whose main aim is to promote the history and theology of Anglicanism as understood by those in the Reformed tradition. Interested readers are welcome to consult its website for further details of its many activities.

The Latimer Trust

London N14 4PS UK

Registered Charity: 1084337

Company Number: 4104465

Web: www.latimertrust.org

E-mail: administrator@latimertrust.org

Introduction

The title of this 2018 St Antholin Lecture introduces us to two large and controversial subjects. One is the man William Perkins and the other is the Reformed doctrine of the church. Perkins has, on the one hand, been lauded by J I Packer as the 'best-known English international theologian' of his generation, joining with John Calvin and Theodore Beza to form 'the trinity of orthodoxy.'[1] On the other hand, Perkins has been portrayed as the leading figure in the decline of Reformed theology—from the vibrant pastures of the Reformation to the arid wastelands of scholasticism.[2] But if Perkins and his theological impact is a controversial subject, no less so is the Reformed doctrine of the church. Indeed, the great seventeenth-century Reformed theologian of Geneva, Francis Turretin, went so far as to say: 'scarcely any other among the controversies waged between us and our opponents in this miserable age ... seems to be of greater moment and more necessary than the disputation concerning the church.'[3] Why does Turretin speak like this? Well, because when we are talking about the church, we are talking about the bride of Christ. And as Geddes MacGregor has said, 'when the divines argued about the Church, they felt they were arguing about that which is closest to Christ and inseparable from him ... Christ and the Church were [not only] two correlative ideas; it was, rather, that they were, in the eyes of these divines, one living reality.'[4] The doctrine of the church matters because she is the bride of Christ.

And because the church matters, debates abound on every side. How can it be known that the Reformed are 'true' churches in distinction from Rome? How should Reformed churches be governed—should they be

---

[1] J.I. Packer, *An Anglican to Remember - William Perkins: Puritan Popularizer* (London: St Antholin's Lectureship Charity Lecture, 1996), 1.
[2] For example, R.T. Kendal, *Calvin and English Calvinism to 1649* (Oxford: Oxford University Press, 1979).
[3] Francis Turretin, *Institutes of Elenctic Theology* (ed. James T. Dennison Jr.: trans. George Musgrave Giger; 3 vols.; Philipsburg: P&R Publishing, 1992) 3:1 (18.1.1).
[4] Geddes MacGregor, *Corpus Christi: The Nature of the Church According to the Reformed Tradition* (London: MacMillan, 1959), 22.

Episcopal, Presbyterian or Congregational? What of the sacraments, who should they be administered to? What of church discipline? What of the role of the clergy as opposed to the laity?[5] What of worship—how is it to be regulated, and what are its most fundamental elements? How does the church relate to the state? Such questions have split churches and divided brothers and sisters in Christ.

Two large and controversial subjects then. But, I trust two hopeful and timely subjects. J I Packer concluded his 1996 St Antholin Lecture on William Perkins saying, 'is there not an uncanny relevancy for us in the thought about ... the Church of England that we have just found Perkins expressing?'[6] There was—and 20 years later, there still is. Perkins' views are still worth hearing. Today's evangelicals are fragmented and divided. As every year goes by, new denominations and new divisions appear. This trend, I am convinced, will only reverse when we return to a robust and biblical definition of the church, to an ecclesiology which is not shot through with post-Enlightenment individualism. As such, it is a key contention of this lecture that a Reformed doctrine of the church, such as that articulated by Perkins, is a real need of the hour.

In tackling this subject, a short biography of Perkins will be provided. Then some general outline of Reformed thinking on the nature of the church will be given, principally through considering the teaching of the Reformed confessions and Calvin. Finally, Perkins' views will be considered, showing how and why he thought that the Church of England was 'a true church of God.'[7]

---

[5] Not all Reformed theologians are comfortable with such a distinction between clergy and laity. See, for example, George Gillespie, *An Assertion of the Government of the Church of Scotland* (Edinburgh: Printed for James Bryson, 1641), 3.

[6] Packer, *An Anglican to Remember*, 21.

[7] William Perkins, *The Works of William Perkins* (eds. Joel R. Beeke and Derek W.H. Thomas; 10 vols.; Grand Rapids, Reformation Heritage Books, 2014-), 4:421 [hereafter Perkins, *Works*]. Where a work has been republished in this edition, I have generally taken my citation from it.

The life and times of William Perkins

The life of William Perkins spanned the Elizabethan era.[8] He was born in 1558, the year Queen Elizabeth ascended to the throne. He died in 1602, the year before the death of Elizabeth. Perkins is thus an Elizabethan man. As such, his life is inevitably shaped and moulded by the political and ecclesiastical context of Elizabethan England. Elizabeth inherited a nation recovering from the changes and persecution which had arisen due to the differences between the strong Protestantism of Edward VI ('England's Josiah') and the Roman Catholicism of Mary I ('Bloody Mary'). It is perhaps right to say that through Elizabeth's astute dealings with 'the entrenched factions ... [she] turned England into the foremost Protestant power by the time of her death in 1603.'[9] However, Elizabeth's ecclesiastical stance was problematic for those Marian exiles

---

[8] For Perkins' life, see, for example, Samuel Clarke, *The Marrow of Ecclesiastical History: Contained in the Lives of One Hundred Forty Eight Fathers, Schoolmen, First Reformers, and Modern Divines which have Flourished in the Church since Christ's Time to this Present Age* (London, 1654), 850-3; Thomas Fuller, *The Holy State and the Profane State* (repr.; London: Thomas Tegg, 1841), 80-83; Bryan D. Spinks, *Two Faces of Elizabethan Anglican Theology: Sacraments and Salvation in the Thought of William Perkins and Richard Hooker* (London: The Scarecrow Press, 1999), 21-37; Packer, *An Anglican to Remember*; Michael Jinkins, 'William Perkins (1558-1602)' in *Oxford Dictionary of National Biography* (online ed., http://www.oxforddnb.com) (Oxford: Oxford University Press); Joel R. Beeke and Randal J. Pederson, *Meet the Puritans* (Grand Rapids: Reformation Heritage Books), 469-480; Joel R. Beeke and Stephen J. Yuile, 'Biographical Introduction' in Perkins, *Works*, ix-xxxii. For general introductions to the times, focusing on the ecclesiastical conflicts, see, for example, W.B. Patterson, *William Perkins and the Making of a Protestant England* (Oxford: Oxford University Press, 2014), 6-39; Peter Lake, *Anglicans and Puritans? Presbyterian and English Conformist Thought from Whitgift to Hooker* (London: Unwin Hyman, 1988); Peter Lake, *Moderate Puritans and the Elizabethan Church* (Cambridge: Cambridge University Press, 1982); Patrick Collinson, The Elizabethan Puritan Movement, (London, 1967); Peter Lake and Michael Questier (eds.), *Conformity and Orthodoxy in the English Church, c. 1560-1660* (Woodbridge: Boydell Press, 2000); Patrick Collinson, *Richard Bancroft and Elizabethan Anti-Puritanism* (Cambridge: Cambridge University Press, 2013).
[9] Beeke and Yuile, 'Biographical Introduction' in Perkins, *Works*, ix.

who had seen, as they deemed it, a purer Protestantism on the continent, and particularly perhaps in Geneva. There were therefore pushes for further reform in liturgy, the area of clerical vestments, and even to move church government in a Presbyterian direction. Some of this reforming mind would go so far as to say, 'we in England are so far off from having a church rightly reformed according to the prescript of God's word, that as yet we are not come to the outward face of the same.'[10] It is this spirit that would lead to the ordinance calling the seventeenth-century Westminster Assembly to speak of the need for 'a more perfect reformation than hath yet been attained' and to designate 'the present Church-government' as 'evil.'[11] It is noticeable that Perkins avoided becoming embroiled in these disputes, and instead laboured to vindicate the Church of England as a true, reformed church.[12]

Perkins was born in Marston Jabbet (near Coventry) in Warwickshire. Little is known of his life before he entered Christ's College, Cambridge, in 1577 at the age of 19. A key figure at Christ's was Laurence Chaderton, an advocate of moderate reform of the Church of England.[13] Perkins would go on to form a close bond with Chaderton and they shared many similar views. Quite how Perkins lived his student years is unknown. But anecdotes tell of 'drunken Perkins.'[14] It is recounted that 'Quickly the wild fire of his youth began to break out ... It is not certain whether his own disposition, or the bad company of others betrayed him to these

---

[10] R. Tudor Jones, ed., *Protestant Nonconformist Texts: Volume 1,1550-1700* (Aldershot: Ashgate, 2007), 37.

[11] *Westminster Confession of Faith* (Glasgow: Free Presbyterian Publications, 1994), 13.

[12] Thus, it is right to say that 'He belonged to no one party in the Church of England, but saw himself as a Church of England man.' Ian Breward, 'Introduction' in William Perkins, *The Works of William Perkins* (Ian Breward, ed.; Appleford: Sutton Courtenay Press, 1970), 113.

[13] For Chadderton, see Joel R. Beeke, 'Laurence Chadderton: An Early Puritan Vision for Church and School' in *Church and School in Early Modern Protestantism: Studies in Honour of Richard A. Muller* (Jordan Baylor, David Systsma and Jason Zuidema, eds.; Leiden: Brill, 2013), 321-338.

[14] Spinks, *Two Faces of Elizabethan Anglican Theology*, 21.

extravagancies.'[15] Clarke notes 'he was very wild in his youth, but the Lord in mercy was pleased to reclaim him.'[16]

At some point in his student days, Perkins was converted and his life was transformed. Clarke would say of Perkins' life after his conversion, 'he was so pious, and spotless, that malice was afraid to bite at his credit, into which she knew that her teeth could not enter.'[17] This is the very testimony a Puritan life was aiming to elicit.[18] Perkins graduated with a BA in 1581, and an MA in 1584, and upon his graduation took up a fellowship at Christ's College.[19] Around this time, Perkins began to preach to the prisoners of the Castle Jail in Cambridge. Clarke recounts that the prisoners were brought out 'fettered as they were' to hear Perkins, and that his preaching freed many of them 'from the captivity of sin, which was their worst bondage.'[20]

The same year, Perkins also became lecturer (preacher) at St Andrew the Great. He was recognised as a powerful preacher. Clarke notes, 'His sermons were not so plain, but the piously learned did admire them; nor so learned, but the plain did not understand them.'[21] Perkins' preaching did see a development through his ministry, with the emphasis shifting from wrath to grace. It was observed that 'In his sermons he used to pronounce the word "damn" with such an emphasis, as left a doleful echo in his auditors' ears a good while after ... But in his old age he was

---

[15] Thomas Fuller, *Abel Redivivus: Or, The Dead Yet Speaking - The Lives and Deaths of the Moderne Divines* (London, 1651), 432, as cited in Spinks, *Two Faces of Elizabethan Anglican Theology*, 21.

[16] Clarke, *Marrow of Ecclesiastical History*, 850. The 'wildness' may have extended to fathering a child outside of marriage. Jinkins, 'William Perkins', ODNB. (Throughout spelling has been modernised.)

[17] Clarke, *Marrow of Ecclesiastical History*, 851.

[18] Thus, Perkins comments, 'Who are so much branded with the vile terms of Puritans and Precisians, as those who most endeavour to get and keep purity of heart in a good conscience.' (Perkins, *Works*, 1:205.) Perkins did not like the name of Puritan, carrying as it did connotations of a schismatic and separatist spirit. Packer, *An Anglican to Remember*, 3.

[19] Spinks, *Two Faces of Elizabethan Anglican Theology*, 22.

[20] Clarke, *Marrow of Ecclesiastical History*, 851.

[21] Clarke, *Marrow of Ecclesiastical History*, 851.

more mild, often professing that to preach mercy is the proper office of ministers of the gospel.'[22]

That desire to preach mercy is perhaps best seen in a well-known anecdote from Perkins' life. It is recounted that Perkins used 'to go with the prisoners to the place of execution when they were condemned.'[23] On one occasion, 'a young lusty fellow' was going up the ladder to his death, but 'he looked with a rueful and heavy countenance, as if he had been half dead already.'[24] Perkins, seeing the young man was utterly unprepared to die, called him to come down. The story continues: 'Whereupon the prisoner coming down, Master Perkins took him by the hand and made him kneel down with himself at the ladder foot, hand in hand, when that blessed man of God made such an effectual prayer in confession of sins ... as made the poor prisoner burst out into abundance of tears ... he proceeded to the second part of his prayer, and therein to show him the Lord Jesus ... stretching forth his blessed hand of mercy, and power to save him.'[25] The happy outcome was that the young man was enabled 'to look beyond death, with the eyes of Faith, to see how the black lines of all his sins were crossed, and cancelled by the red lines of his crucified Saviour's precious blood ... [he] went up the ladder again so comforted, and took his death with ... patience and alacrity.'[26] This shows us, as well as anything can, the heart of Perkins. Perkins never forgot that, 'pure and undefiled religion before God and the Father is this: to visit orphans and widows in their trouble, and to keep oneself unspotted from the world' (James 1:27, NKJV).

As well as his preaching and his college fellowship, Perkins fulfilled other duties in the University. Beeke and Peterson note, 'He was Dean of Christ's College from 1590-1591. He catechised the students at Corpus Christi College on Thursday afternoons, lecturing on the Ten Commandments ... On Sunday afternoons, he worked as an advisor,

---

[22] Clarke, *Marrow of Ecclesiastical History*, 851.
[23] Clarke, *Marrow of Ecclesiastical History*, 852.
[24] Clarke, *Marrow of Ecclesiastical History*, 852.
[25] Clarke, *Marrow of Ecclesiastical History*, 853.
[26] Clarke, *Marrow of Ecclesiastical History*, 853.

counselling the spiritually distressed.'[27] Perkins influenced many who would go on to have significant ministries of their own, for example, Richard Sibbes, John Cotton, John Preston and William Ames. Ames' testimony may suffice: 'I gladly call to mind the time, when being young I heard worthy Master Perkins so preach in a great assembly of students, that he instructed them soundly in the truth, stirred them up to seek after godliness, [and] made them fit for the kingdom of God.'[28]

Perkins was not just a busy figure in Cambridge. He was also a scholar of international repute. Clarke tell us that Perkins, 'had a rare felicity in reading of books, and as it were but turning them over, would give an exact account of all that was considerable therein. He perused books so speedily that one would think he read nothing, and yet so accurately that one would think he read all.'[29] As such, Perkins was very familiar with Reformed theologians, including Calvin, Bucer, Bullinger, Musculus, Beza, Zanchius, Olevianus and Peter Martyr.[30] His theological learning led Perkins, rightly, to be called, 'easily the most pre-eminent English churchman and theologian of his remarkable generation.'[31]

Perkins' writings were collected in three large volumes and are currently being reprinted by Reformation Heritage Books in ten volumes.[32] Some of his most influential works include:

---

[27] Beeke and Pederson, *Meet the Puritans*, 471.

[28] William Ames, 'To the Reader,' in *Conscience with the Power and Cases Thereof* (London, 1643), as cited in Beeke and Yuile, 'Biographical Introduction' in Perkins, *Works*, xiii.

[29] Clarke, *Marrow of Ecclesiastical History*, 851.

[30] Spinks, *Two Faces of Elizabethan Anglican Theology*, 26; Packer, *An Anglican to Remember*, 18; Jinkins, 'William Perkins', ODNB.

[31] Philip Benedict, *Christ's Churches Purely Reformed: A Social History of Calvinism* (New Haven: Yale University Press, 2002), 319. Thus, Patterson comments, 'Perkins was the best known English theologian in Continental Europe in his lifetime and for several decades afterwards.' Patterson, *William Perkins*, 88.

[32] William Perkins, *The Workes of that famous and Worthy Minister of Christ in the University of Cambridge, Mr William Perkins* (3 vols.; London: John Legatt,

- *The Foundation of Christian Religion* (1590), a popular summary of Christian principles
- *A Golden Chain* (1591), a presentation of supralapsarian predestinarian theology[33]
- *A Case of Conscience, the Greatest that Ever Was: How a Man May Know Whether he be the Child of God or No* (1592)
- *The Art of Prophesying* (1592), on the nature and task of preaching
- *An Exposition of the Symbol or Creed of the Apostles* (1595)
- *A Reformed Catholic* (1597), a defence of Protestant churches as against Rome

In his day, he was a popular writer and Packer notes, 'No Puritan author save Richard Baxter ever sold better than Perkins.'[34] Patrick Collinson calls Perkins, 'the prince of Puritan theologians and the most eagerly read.'[35] Packer believed that 'Perkins' special strength ... was to be systematic, scholarly, solid and simple at the same time.'[36] He goes on to comment that Perkins' works were soon translated into French, Dutch, Italian, Spanish, Czech, German, Hungarian, Latin and Welsh! William Haller has said, 'No books, it is fair to say, were more often to be found on the shelves of succeeding generations of preachers, and the name of no preacher recurs more often in later Puritan literature.'[37] It was the success of his writings that really cemented Perkins' reputation, and

---

1626-1631) [hereafter, Perkins, *Works (1626-1631)*]. References to the modern edition are noted Perkins, *Works*.

[33] Packer is surely right to say, 'Most seventeenth-century Puritans, like most Reformed theologians since their time were infralapsarian, and it is in order, I think, to express quiet regret the Perkins the Elizabethan Puritan pioneer took a different line.' Packer, *An Anglican to Remember*, 20.

[34] Packer, *An Anglican to Remember*, 1. Beeke and Pederson note that 'By the time of his death Perkins's writings in England were outselling those of Calvin, Beza, and Bullinger combined.' Beeke and Pederson, *Meet the Puritans*, 473-74.

[35] Collinson, *The Elizabethan Puritan Movement*, 125. For the reception of Perkins' writings, see Patterson, *William Perkins*, 190-196.

[36] Packer, *An Anglican to Remember*, 3.

[37] William Haller, *The Rise of Puritanism* (New York: Columbia University Press, 1938), 65, as cited in Packer, *An Anglican to Remember*, 3. Granting a degree of overstatement, it remains a powerful testimony.

entitles him to be placed at the head of the movement of Puritanism in the seventeenth century. It is true that 'he set the tone for the seventeenth-century Puritan accent on Reformed, experiential truth and self-examination, and their polemic against Roman Catholicism and Arminianism.'[38]

So, Perkins the theologian. What of Perkins the man? As to Perkins' character, in so far as we can make anything of it, we have to rely on Clarke who tells us 'He was of a cheerful nature, and pleasant disposition. Somewhat reserved to strangers, but when once acquainted, very familiar.'[39] If that was his character, Clarke's description of Perkins' physical appearance is more amusing, and less complimentary, 'He was of a ruddy complexion, fat, and corpulent. Lame of his right hand, yet this Ehud with a left-handed pen did stab the Romish cause.'[40]

Perkins married Timothye Cradock of Grantchester in 1595, and because of that he had to give up his Fellowship at Christ's. Wealthy supporters added to his income as lecturer in St Andrew the Great to ensure his ministry there would continue.[41] In his seven years of marriage, Perkins had seven children, three of whom died in infancy.[42] Having served his whole career in Cambridge, he died in 1602, aged 44 of unrelieved gallstones.[43] Dr James Montague (afterwards Bishop of Bath and Wells) preached his funeral sermon on the text, 'Moses my servant is dead.'[44] Perkins' influence in Cambridge lasted many years, with Thomas Goodwin arriving in Cambridge ten years after Perkins' death

---

[38] Beeke and Pederson, *Meet the Puritans*, 473.
[39] Clarke, *Marrow of Ecclesiastical History*, 851.
[40] Clarke, *Marrow of Ecclesiastical History*, 852.
[41] Packer, *An Anglican to Remember*, 2.
[42] Packer, *An Anglican to Remember*, 2.
[43] Packer, *An Anglican to Remember*, 2.
[44] Clarke, *Marrow of Ecclesiastical History*, 852.

proclaiming 'the town was then filled with the discourse of the power of Mr Perkins, his ministry still fresh in men's memories.'[45]

Despite being noted as the fountainhead of Puritanism, Perkins lived all his days as a faithful son of the Church of England. As R T Kendall notes, 'he saw himself as being in the mainstream of the Church of England, which he often defended.'[46] When we come to consider his doctrine of the church, we will see why. Perkins, as far as can be ascertained, had two main brushes with the church authorities. One was in 1587 when Perkins, as described by Spinks, 'had to answer for a sermon preached in Christ's Chapel in which it is alleged that he was critical of kneeling for reception, facing east, and the practice of the minister administering the communion elements to himself. He was, however, able to acquit himself of any serious censure, and the Consistory accepted his account of the matter.'[47] Perkins confessed that he 'might have spoken at a more convenient time' and the matter was at an end.[48] He was also on the fringes of a movement which sought to operate a shadow Presbyterian system alongside conformity to the government of the Church of England. In 1591, he was questioned under oath on this—particularly regarding a quasi-Presbyterian meeting he had attended in September 1589. Perkins said that he did not 'know that any minister did at any time meet at any place to the purpose to conclude, debate or order how the said discipline might be advanced or practised.'[49] While some have reacted to this claim with incredulity, Spinks notes that 'it may well be that he simply attended the Cambridge meetings by invitation for his opinion

---

[45] Robert Halley, 'Memoir of Thomas Goodwin,' in *The Works of Thomas Goodwin, Volume 2* (Edinburgh: James Nichol, 1861), xiii. For a summary of other similar testimonies, see Patterson, *William Perkins*, 196-215.

[46] Kendall, *Calvin and English Calvinism to 1649*, 54.

[47] Spinks, *Two Faces of Elizabethan Anglican Theology*, 4.

[48] Spinks, *Two Faces of Elizabethan Anglican Theology*, 22; Patterson, *William Perkins*, 46-47.

[49] As cited in Breward, ed., *The Works of William Perkins*, 10.

and advice and probably had little interest ... in terms of dates and personages.'[50]

Despite these minor brushes with authority, it is right to note that 'in his day he was regarded as authentically "Anglican" as Hooker, insofar as that term had any meaning in the Elizabethan church.'[51] Packer helpfully summarises that Perkins was content to endure 'ecclesiastical inconvenience for the time being in order to fulfil in the Church of England a full-scale soul-saving ministry.'[52] Perkins, however, did what he could to protect those within the church who were attacked by the anti-Puritans.[53] For example, he defended Francis Johnson, also of Christ's College, when he was imprisoned for favouring Presbyterian church government and his preface to his *Golden Chain* (1590) shows that he was not in favour of Archbishop Whitgift's suppression of Puritanism.[54] Nevertheless, despite this, 'he remained a devoted defender of the essential doctrines and liturgical practices of the Church of England.'[55]

'The' Reformed doctrine of the church

So, that is Perkins' life. But before turning to Perkins' thought on the church, some further context needs to be given. What did Reformed theologians up to Perkins' time make of the doctrine of the church? Did they think of the church in a consistent manner? Without the constraints of time and space, this topic could take up several volumes. So, necessarily, what can be said will be a highly condensed summary,

---

[50] Spinks, *Two Faces of Elizabethan Anglican Theology*, 23. See also Patterson, William Perkins, 47-48.
[51] Spinks, *Two Faces of Elizabethan Anglican Theology*, 5.
[52] J.I. Packer, *Puritan Portraits* (Fearn: Christian Focus, 2012), 133.
[53] He was conscious that many spoke of 'the heresy of Puritanism'. Perkins, 'A Commentarie upon the Epistle to the Galatians', in *Works (1626-31)*, 2:318.
[54] Jinkins, 'William Perkins', ODNB.
[55] Jinkins, 'William Perkins', ODNB. This could still involve him in controversy. For example, his *Golden Chain* was a response to the predestinarian views of Peter Baro (Lady Margaret's Professor of Divinity).

focusing on how the confessional statements of Reformed churches and one leading theologian, John Calvin, defined and identified the church of Jesus Christ.

Reformed confessions and catechisms

From the early days, Reformed churches, having separated from Rome, had to face the question, 'What is the church?' If it is not found in communion with Rome, where is it found, how is it defined, and what does is mean, having separated from Rome, to continue to confess, 'I believe in the holy catholic Church'?[56] Various Reformed confessions addressed this and they will now be considered in turn.

The **First Helvetic Confession** (1536) articulated a clear distinction in the definition of the church into a pure church of the saved, known only to God, and an institutional, visible, earthly church. The creed defined the church as 'the holy gathering of all the saints, and the immaculate bride of Christ.'[57] This is the church of God's saved, redeemed people. The church of those whose names are written in the Lamb's book of life. But the First Helvetic goes on to say that the church under this ideal definition is 'known only to the eyes of God.'[58] However, the true church still can be 'discerned and known' by 'certain external rights, instituted by Christ himself and by the Word of God, for instance, public and legitimate discipline.'[59]

The **Geneva Confession** (1537) expanded on how a true visible church can be identified. It stated that 'the proper mark for discerning the church of Jesus Christ is that his holy gospel is faithfully preached there ... [and] that

---

[56] *The Apostles' Creed* in Philip Schaff, *The Creeds of Christendom* (3 vols.; 1931.; Repr., Grand Rapids: Baker, 1993), 2:45. The use of 'catholic' here is in the sense of universal, rather then in the sense of Roman Catholic.

[57] 'The First Helvetic Confession' in James Dennison, ed., *Reformed Confessions of the Sixteenth and Seventeenth Centuries* (4 vols.; Grand Rapids: Reformation Heritage Books, 2008-2014), 1:347.

[58] 'The First Helvetic Confession' in Dennison, *Reformed Confessions*, 1:347.

[59] 'The First Helvetic Confession' in Dennison, *Reformed Confessions*, 1:347.

his sacraments are rightly administered.'[60] So already, in the mid-1530s, twenty years or so after the Ninety-Five Theses, we can see church discipline (First Helvetic Confession), the preaching of the Word and right administration of the sacraments (Geneva Confession) being the marks of a visible church that is a true church. Without these, the Geneva Confession said, 'we do not recognise the form of the church at all.'[61] But there is one important addition. The Geneva Confession goes on to remind us, as the Helvetic did, that in a true church 'there may be some imperfections and faults, as there always will be among men.'[62]

While other confessions (for example, the **French Confession**) continued to include ways to identify the church, perhaps the clearest articulation of the Reformed view is found in the **Scots Confession** of 1560.[63] The Confession declared that 'we most constantly believe that from the beginning there has been, now is, and to the end of the world shall be, a kirk: that is to say, a company and multitude of men chosen of God, who rightly worship and embrace him, by true faith in Christ Jesus.'[64] This church 'is catholic—that is, universal—because it contains the elect of all ages, all realms, nations, and tongues, be they of the Jews, or be they of the Gentiles; who have communion and society with God the Father, and with his Son Christ Jesus, through the sanctification of his Holy Spirit.'[65] To be outside this church is to be unsaved, 'out of the which kirk there is neither life, nor eternal felicity.'[66] However, in speaking in these terms, the Scots Confession is speaking of the ideal church of the saved, the invisible church: 'This kirk is invisible, known only to God, who alone knows whom he has chosen, and comprehends as well (as is said) the

---

[60] 'Geneva Confession (1536/37)' in Dennison, *Reformed Confessions*, 1:400.
[61] 'Geneva Confession (1536/37)' in Dennison, *Reformed Confessions*, 1:400.
[62] 'Geneva Confession (1536/37)' in Dennison, *Reformed Confessions*, 1:400.
[63] 'The French Confession (1559)' in Dennison, *Reformed Confessions*, 2:149-50.
[64] 'The Scottish Confession' in Dennison, *Reformed Confessions*, 2:197.
[65] 'The Scottish Confession' in Dennison, *Reformed Confessions*, 2:197.
[66] 'The Scottish Confession' in Dennison, *Reformed Confessions*, 2:197. As will be seen this language can also be employed with regard to the true visible church, as Calvin does, for example.

elect that are departed (commonly called the kirk triumphant), as those that yet live and fight against sin and Satan as shall live hereafter.'[67]

But fellowship cannot be had with an invisible church, it must be had with a visible church. So how is it known if a visible church is a true church of Jesus Christ? The Scots Confession sees this as an important question, for 'Satan from the beginning has laboured to deck his pestilent synagogue with the title of the kirk of God ... [therefore] it is a thing most requisite that the true kirk be discerned from the filthy synagogue, by clear and perfect notes, lest we, being deceived, receive and embrace to our own condemnation the one for the other.'[68] What then are the 'notes, signs, and assured tokens whereby the immaculate spouse of Christ Jesus is known from that horrible harlot, the kirk malignant'?[69] They are not 'antiquity, title usurped, lineal descent, place appointed, nor multitude of men approving an error.'[70] Rather, 'The notes ... of the true kirk of God we believe, confess, and avow to be: first, the true preaching of the Word of God, into the which God has revealed himself to us, as the writings of the prophets and apostles do declare; secondly, the right administration of the sacraments of Christ Jesus, which must be annexed unto the Word and promise of God, to seal and confirm the same in our hearts; last, ecclesiastical discipline uprightly ministered, as God's Word prescribes, whereby vice is repressed, and virtue nourished.'[71] The Scots Confession went on to state that 'Wheresoever then these former notes are seen, and of any time continue (be the number never so few, about two or three) there, without all doubt, is the true kirk of Christ ... such as were in Corinth, Galatia, Ephesus, and other places in which the ministry was planted by Paul, and were of himself named the kirks of God.'[72]

---

[67] 'The Scottish Confession' in Dennison, *Reformed Confessions*, 2:197-98.

[68] 'The Scottish Confession' in Dennison, *Reformed Confessions*, 2:198.

[69] 'The Scottish Confession' in Dennison, *Reformed Confessions*, 2:198.

[70] 'The Scottish Confession' in Dennison, *Reformed Confessions*, 2:198.

[71] 'The Scottish Confession' in Dennison, *Reformed Confessions*, 2:198-9.

[72] 'The Scottish Confession' in Dennison, *Reformed Confessions*, 2:199. The Scots Confession obviously included the Church of Scotland in the list of true churches, 'And such kirks we, the inhabitants of the realm of Scotland, professors of Christ Jesus, confess ourselves to have in our cities, towns, and

The teaching of the Scots Confession is expanded on in **Craig's Catechism** (1581), a popular catechism in Scotland. The Catechism stated that the church confessed in the Apostles' Creed is 'the whole company of God's elect called and sanctified.'[73] This church is, in classic terms, 'invisible' as 'it contains only God's elect, known only to himself.'[74] Nevertheless, the true church may be known in visible form. It is identified by 'the true profession of the Word and holy sacraments.'[75] If these two marks are lacking, 'they are not the holy church of God.'[76] However, if these marks were present then it was not permissible to leave a church, 'albeit sundry other vices abound.'[77] Even where 'the multitude are wicked and profane' still there 'is a true church where the Word truly remains' because 'the infallible token of Christ's church' is nothing but 'the word truly preached and professed.'[78] That the faithful 'are joined with the wicked in the body' does not hurt or damage them for, 'we and they are spiritually separated.'[79] The participation of the wicked in the sacraments likewise does not make the sacraments less spiritually helpful to the faithful.[80] This kind of teaching illustrates the importance of church unity, and the high bar placed before separation from a church could be justified.

The teaching of the **Thirty-Nine Articles** (1563) follows the broad outline of Reformed confessions considered so far. They state: 'The visible church of Christ is a congregation of faithful men, in which the pure Word of God is preached and the sacraments be duly administered according to Christ's ordinance.'[81] Here, the Thirty-Nine Articles list the

---

places reformed; for the doctrine taught in our kirks is contained in the written Word of God.'

[73] 'Craig's Catechism' in Dennison, *Reformed Confessions*, 3:563. This is in contrast to Calvin, who acknowledged the Apostles' Creed spoke of the visible church.

[74] 'Craig's Catechism' in Dennison, *Reformed Confessions*, 3:563.

[75] 'Craig's Catechism' in Dennison, *Reformed Confessions*, 3:565.

[76] 'Craig's Catechism' in Dennison, *Reformed Confessions*, 3:565.

[77] 'Craig's Catechism' in Dennison, *Reformed Confessions*, 3:565.

[78] 'Craig's Catechism' in Dennison, *Reformed Confessions*, 3:565.

[79] 'Craig's Catechism' in Dennison, *Reformed Confessions*, 3:565.

[80] 'Craig's Catechism' in Dennison, *Reformed Confessions*, 3:565.

[81] 'The Thirty-Nine Articles' in Dennison, *Reformed Confessions*, 2:760-1.

preaching of the Word and right administration of the sacraments as the marks of the church. Discipline is not included, but this was not uncommon for, as will now be considered, Calvin did not regard it as a necessary mark of the church either.

John Calvin

So far, the confessional teaching that the true visible Church is known by the true preaching of the Word, the right administration of the sacraments and, for most, by discipline. Before moving on to William Perkins' doctrine of the true Church, a brief summary of Calvin's teaching will be given, as their views have much in common. It needs to be said at the outset how highly Calvin regarded the visible church. He stated:

> It is now our intention to discuss the visible church, let us learn even from the simple title 'mother' how ... necessary it is that we should know her. For there is no other way to enter into life unless this mother conceive us in her womb, give us birth, nourish us at her breast, and lastly, unless she keep us under her care and guidance until, putting off mortal flesh, we become like the angels.'[82]

Like the Reformed creeds, Calvin distinguished between the visible and invisible church. He noted that church could be taken to mean 'those who are children of God by grace of adoption', and in this sense the church is 'invisible to us, [and] is visible to the eyes of God alone.'[83] By contrast, the visible church 'designated the whole multitude of men spread over the earth who profess to worship one God by Christ' and as such 'in this church are mingled many hypocrites who have nothing of Christ but the

---

[82] John Calvin, *Institutes of the Christian Religion* (ed. John T. McNeill; trans. Ford Lewis Battles; 2 vols.; Louisville: Westminster John Knox), 2:1016 (4.1.4). There is something tremendously beautiful about this statement of Calvin's.
[83] Calvin, *Institutes*, 2:1021-22 (4.1.7).

name and outward appearance.'[84] Despite the mixed condition of the visible church, it was possible to identify a true visible church.

For Calvin, the marks of this true church are, 'the word of God purely preached and heard, and the sacraments administered according to Christ's institution.'[85] Where these are present, 'it is not to be doubted, a church of God exists.'[86] Calvin was resolutely opposed to leaving a church which had these marks, arguing 'how deadly a temptation it is, when one is prompted to withdraw from a congregation wherein are seen the signs and tokens with which the Lord thought his church sufficiently marked.'[87] He argued that even where 'some faults may creep into the administration of doctrine or sacraments, this ought not to estrange us from communion with the church.'[88] He distinguished between fundamental doctrines (for example, the Trinity) and 'other articles of doctrine disputed which still do not break the unity of the faith.'[89] If Calvin warned against overzealousness for secondary doctrines leading to breaches in the visible church, he was even more opposed to failures in church discipline leading to church divisions. He criticised those who 'when they do not see a quality of life corresponding to the doctrine of the gospel among those to whom it is announced, they immediately judge that no church exists in that place.'[90] Calvin argued that 'they are vainly seeking a church besmirched with no blemish.'[91] He noted that the church in Corinth suffered from 'corruption not only of morals but of doctrine' and yet was still regarded by Paul as a true church.[92] More could be said here, but to summarise. Calvin had a high view of the visible church, but he recognised its failings. However, these did not warrant schism, as long as the fundamentals of sound doctrine were maintained.

---

[84] Calvin, *Institutes*, 2:1021 (4.1.7).
[85] Calvin, *Institutes*, 2:1023 (4.1.9)
[86] Calvin, *Institutes*, 2:1023 (4.1.9).
[87] Calvin, *Institutes*, 2:1025 (4.1.11).
[88] Calvin, *Institutes*, 2:1025 (4.1.12).
[89] Calvin, *Institutes*, 2:1026 (4.1.12).
[90] Calvin, *Institutes*, 2:1027 (4.1.13).
[91] Calvin, *Institutes*, 2:1028 (4.1.13)
[92] Calvin, *Institutes*, 2:1028 (4.1.14).

Summary

To conclude on the Reformed teaching on the nature of the church, we can look to Ian Hazlett's helpful summary. He rightly notes that, for the Reformed, 'the true church is invisible ... the spiritual convocation of elect individuals, past, present and future.'[93] This leads on to a distinction between this church and the visible church: 'the invisible and visible churches were not identical; the former an object of faith, the latter a societal body in which there can be faked faith.'[94] Nevertheless, there is overlap, and 'the two churches may still coincide.'[95] The visible church is a true church, Hazlett notes, when 'the formal marks of a proper church [which] where usually seen as threefold' existed, namely 'preaching, two sacraments and church discipline.'[96] However, Hazlett rightly notes that 'the third [mark], discipline, was not always formally cited as a mark.'[97] It was possible for a church to exist without discipline while, 'preaching and the sacraments ... constitute the Church; without them there can be no church.'[98] But even here there is a rank, and the 'one "necessary and perpetual mark" of the church' was 'the Word and orthodox doctrine.'[99]

William Perkins and the Reformed doctrine of the church

The invisible church

So, this is the doctrine of the church that Perkins inherited. A pure invisible church known only to God, and a true visible church known by two or three marks: the preaching of the word, the right administration of the sacraments and church discipline. Perkins himself embraced the classic Reformed definition of the church as invisible and visible. Taking Jude 1 as starting point, 'called, sanctified by God the Father, and

---

[93] Ian Hazlett, 'Church and Church/State Relations' in U.L. Lerner, R.A. Muller, A. G. Roeber (eds.), *The Oxford Handbook of Early Modern Theology, 1600-1800* (Oxford: Oxford University Press, 2016), 244.
[94] Hazlett, 'Church and Church/State Relations,' 244.
[95] Hazlett, 'Church and Church/State Relations,' 244.
[96] Hazlett, 'Church and Church/State Relations,' 245.
[97] Hazlett, 'Church and Church/State Relations,' 245.
[98] Hazlett, 'Church and Church/State Relations,' 246.
[99] Hazlett, 'Church and Church/State Relations,' 246.

preserved in Jesus Christ', Perkins says this is a definition of the 'militant catholic church.'[100] On this view, the church consists of 'the number of believers dispersed through the face of the whole world, who are effectually called and sanctified and reserved unto life everlasting.'[101] In other words, for Perkins, this church consists of 'only the elect, such as are chosen unto life everlasting ... the church of the "firstborn" (Hebrews 12:23), whose names are written in the Book of Life.'[102] This church is one across time (Old and New Testaments), locations (different nations) and in earth (militant) and in heaven (triumphant).[103] This church is unknown to us, for 'Christ ... He only knows them who and where they be through the face of the whole earth.'[104] As such, 'this catholic church is invisible and cannot by the eye of flesh be discerned, for what eye ... can see or discern the depth of God's election.'[105] This catholic Church which 'cannot utterly perish and be dissolved' is not identical with any visible church for 'particular churches, being mixed and the greatest part not predestinate, may fail.'[106] Thus the scriptural churches of Ephesus, Corinth and Galatia all ultimately failed and fell while the catholic church 'consisting only of a number elected ... cannot possibly fail.'[107]

---

[100] Perkins, 'Exposition upon the Whole Epistle of Jude,' in *Works*, 4:24.

[101] Perkins, 'Exposition upon the Whole Epistle of Jude,' in *Works*, 4:24. See also, Perkins, 'An Exposition of the Creed,' in *Works*, 5:324, 371.

[102] Perkins, 'Exposition upon the Whole Epistle of Jude,' in *Works*, 4:24-25. See also, Perkins, 'Exposition upon the First Three Chapters of Revelation,' in *Works*, 4:555.

[103] Perkins, 'An Exposition upon the Epistle of Jude,' in *Works (1626-31)*, 3:504. On the church militant and triumphant, see also Perkins, 'An Exposition of the Creed,' in *Works*, 5:373-5.

[104] Perkins, 'Exposition upon the Whole Epistle of Jude,' in *Works*, 4:25. So Patterson rightly comments, 'The Church in this sense is invisible because its members are chosen by and known only to God.' (Patterson, *William Perkins*, 76.)

[105] Perkins, 'Exposition upon the Whole Epistle of Jude,' in *Works*, 4:25. See also, Perkins, 'An Exposition upon the Epistle of Jude,' in *Works (1626-31)*, 3:504.

[106] Perkins, 'Exposition upon the Whole Epistle of Jude,' in *Works*, 4:25.

[107] Perkins, 'Exposition upon the Whole Epistle of Jude,' in *Works*, 4:25.

The visible church

But leaving to one side the invisible church, it is possible to identify a true visible church for Perkins.[108] He argued that as we may know 'whether a man is a true apostle or not ... by the same gift it may discern the state of any particular church.'[109] This was not with the marks that the Roman church used, such as antiquity, apostolic succession and numbers.[110] Rather, a true visible church is known by fidelity to 'the doctrine of the prophets and apostles and obedience thereto, proceeding forward in sanctification.'[111] With this mark present, it can be concluded that a particular church belongs to the 'catholic church.'[112] Perkins stated that 'the doctrine taught by the apostles concerning Christ, is made the foundation of the church, and ... where this doctrine is rightly held and confessed, there it is an infallible note of the true church.'[113] This was not to presume that there would be doctrinal uniformity in a church, just agreement in essential articles of faith. Perkins stated that 'men differ in

---

[108] The invisible church is more or less visible at given points in time. Before the Reformation, Perkins argued, 'universal apostasy overspread the face of the whole earth, and ... our church then was not visible to the world but lay hid under the chaff of popery.' Perkins, 'An Exposition of the Creed,' in *Works*, 5:376-7. As such 'visibility' cannot be the mark of God's church for 'God's church is a company of men which believe. The ground of the church is God's election and adoption and man's faith, which none other can see, but the parties that have them.' Perkins, 'Exposition upon the First Three Chapters of Revelation,' in *Works*, 4:506.

[109] Perkins, 'Exposition upon the First Three Chapters of Revelation,' in *Works*, 4:421.

[110] Perkins, 'Exposition upon the Whole Epistle of Jude,' in *Works*, 4:26. See also Perkins, 'An Exposition upon Christ's Sermon in the Mount,' in *Works (1626-31)*, 3:230.

[111] Perkins, 'Exposition upon the Whole Epistle of Jude,' in *Works*, 4:26. On occasions, Perkins identified suffering as a mark of the true church. For example, Perkins, 'Of The Right Knowledge of Christ Crucified,' in *Works (1626-31)*, 1:628; 'An Exposition of the Creed,' in *Works*, 5:374.

[112] Perkins, 'Exposition upon the Whole Epistle of Jude,' in *Works*, 4:26.

[113] Perkins, 'An Exposition upon Christ's Sermon in the Mount,' in *Works (1626-31)*, 3:62. See also, Perkins, 'An Exposition upon the Epistle of Jude,' in *Works (1626-31)*, 3:577; 'An Exposition of the Creed,' in *Works*, 5:378.

sundry opinions in the true church of God, yet they all agree in the Articles of faith; their difference is in matters beside the foundation.'[114]

The true administration of the sacraments is also a mark of a true visible church. Perkins stated regarding baptism that 'the lawful use thereof is a note, whereby the true church of God is discerned and distinguished from the false church.'[115] Perkins wrote quite beautifully that 'God's true church on earth, where his Word is freely known and preached, and his holy sacraments duly administered ... Let us associate ourselves to this church ... This is the suburbs of heaven; so shall we be ready to enter into the glorious city itself, when the Lord calls us.'[116]

Church discipline was also important as, 'men should not be admitted hand over head to the Lord's table, but scandalous persons ought to be restrained.'[117] This power of discipline was the 'power of the keys' in Matthew 16:19. Faithful use of these keys meant that 'the Word and Sacraments are preserved from pollution and profanation, [and] the souls of men pulled out of the snares of the devil ... which being taken away, there will be no difference left between the Kingdom of God and the kingdom of the Devil.'[118] This exercising of the power of the keys was, for Perkins, a mark of 'the state of a true church.'[119] He explicitly stated that 'the due execution of discipline according to the Word' is necessary to 'the good estate of the church.'[120]

---

[114] Perkins, 'An Exposition upon Christ's Sermon in the Mount,' in *Works (1626-31)*, 3:65.

[115] Perkins, 'Cases of Conscience,' in *Works (1626-31)*, 2:74.

[116] Perkins, 'A Commentarie upon the Eleventh Chapter to the Hebrews,' in *Works (1626-31)*, 3:83.

[117] Perkins, 'An Exposition upon Christ's Sermon in the Mount,' in *Works (1626-31)*, 3:67.

[118] Perkins, 'An Exposition upon the Epistle of Jude,' in *Works (1626-31)*, 3:503. See also Perkins, 'An Exposition Upon the First Three Chapters of Revelation,' in *Works (1626-31)*, 3:341; 'Exposition upon the First Three Chapters of Revelation,' in *Works*, 4:567-73.

[119] Perkins, 'An Exposition upon the Epistle of Jude,' in *Works (1626-31)*, 3:503.

[120] Perkins, 'An Exposition of the Creed,' in *Works*, 5:378. Perkins stated, 'Christ has given to His church a power judicial to suspend evil men from the

The conclusion is therefore correct that 'In dealing with ecclesiastical government Perkins sets out three marks of the Church.'[121] However, the three marks are not equal, as will be seen. Where church discipline is lacking and sin is tolerated in practice in the church, this does not vitiate the existence of the true church.[122] Perkins explicitly says that if the sacraments and church discipline are lacking 'so be it there be preaching of the word with obedience in the people, there is for substance a true church of God.'[123]

The Church of England

Perkins had to apply these marks to his own church, the national Church of England. How did she fare when measured by these marks? For Perkins, judged by this standard, the Church of England of his day, 'we may know ... to be the true visible church of God.'[124] He often acknowledged that this was denied by some. Most often, he had in mind not Rome, but the separatists that were beginning to emerge in England, the most famous being Robert Brown (around 1550-1633). The separatists were arguing that the perceived deficiencies in the Church of England rendered it no true church of Jesus Christ. Perkins knew the accusations that 'it is no church of God, that there are no true ministers, true

sacraments and to excommunicate them from the outward fellowship of the church.' Perkins, 'Exposition upon the First Three Chapters of Revelation,' in *Works*, 4:419. See also, Perkins, 'Exposition upon the First Three Chapters of Revelation,' in *Works*, 4:529.

[121] Patterson, *William Perkins*, 51. See also, Perkins, 'An Exposition of the Creed,' in *Works*, 5:384.

[122] Perkins, 'An Exposition upon Christ's Sermon in the Mount,' in *Works (1626-31)*, 3:67.

[123] Perkins, 'An Exposition of the Creed,' in *Works*, 5:378. See also the comments in Patterson, *William Perkins*, 77. Perkins argues that the presence of the sacraments alone does not make a valid church, for the Samaritans had circumcision, but were not the true Jewish church. Perkins, 'Exposition upon the First Three Chapters of Revelation,' in *Works (1626-31)*, 3:329. In contrast, right doctrine makes a church true, 'the true mark is the doctrine of the Prophets and Apostles truly taught and believed.' Perkins, 'An Exposition upon the Epistle of Jude,' in *Works (1626-31)*, 3:504.

[124] Perkins, 'Exposition upon the Whole Epistle of Jude,' in *Works*, 4:26.

preaching, or right administration of the sacraments in it.'[125] Because of this view, 'sundry men ... do separate themselves from our Church as being no true member of the Church of God.'[126]

Perkins dismissive of these accusations. He proved that 'ours is a true Church of God' by the fact that 'the churches of Germany, France, Scotland, and Italy that have received the gospel are the churches of God; and they have the gift of discerning which is a true church of God and which is not' and these churches 'give the right hand of fellowship unto us and reverence our church as the church of God.'[127] Perkins stated that he would listen to the testimony of these churches rather than 'to the opinion of a few private men' and so the Church of England stood as 'the true Church of God.'[128] He complained that 'great therefore is the rashness and want of moderation in many ... that condemn our church for no church'.[129] He even argued that there were 'greater faults' in those who criticised the Church of England than in the church itself.[130] As such

---

[125] Perkins, 'Exposition upon the First Three Chapters of Revelation,' in *Works*, 4:421. See also, Perkins, 'An Exposition upon Christ's Sermon in the Mount,' in *Works (1626-31)*, 3:240-41; 'Exposition upon the First Three Chapters of Revelation,' in *Works (1626-31)*, 3:286; 'An Exposition of the Creed,' in *Works*, 5:383. For a defence of the ministry of the Church of England against Rome, see *A Treatise of Callings* in *Works (1626-31)*, 1:761-62.

[126] Perkins, 'An Exposition upon Christ's Sermon in the Mount,' in *Works (1626-31)*, 3:65.

[127] Perkins, 'Exposition upon the First Three Chapters of Revelation,' in *Works*, 4:421. See also, Patterson, *William Perkins*, 77. See, Perkins, 'An Exposition of the Creede,' in *Works (1626-31)*, 1:307; 'An Exposition upon Christ's Sermon in the Mount,' in *Works (1626-31)*, 3:65. In turn, Perkins acknowledged that 'the churches of Helvetia and Savoy and the free cities of France and the Low Countries and Scotland are to be reverenced as the true churches of God, as their confessions make manifest.' Perkins, 'An Exposition of the Creed,' in *Works*, 5:383.

[128] Perkins, 'Exposition upon the First Three Chapters of Revelation,' in *Works*, 4:421.

[129] Perkins, 'A Commentaries upon the Epistle to the Galatians,' in *Works (1626-31)*, 2:161.

[130] Perkins, 'A Commentaries upon the Epistle to the Galatians,' in *Works (1626-31)*, 2:161.

critics of the Church of England simply made 'peremptory asseverations, wanting sufficient ground, [and] are but paper shot.'[131] Perkins averred that:

> No man ought to sever himself from the Church of England for some wants that be therein. We have the true doctrine of Christ preached among us by God's blessing, and though there be corruptions in manner among us, yea, and though they could justly find fault with our doctrine, yet so long as we hold Christ, no man ought to sever himself from our Church.[132]

Perkins argued repeatedly that the Church of England embraced apostolic teaching, and therefore possessed this mark of a true church. He stated that 'the doctrine touching Christ held and received in our churches, is confirmed by the testimonies of the Prophets and Apostles, and therefore for substance and doctrine is theirs.'[133] As noted above, Perkins held that 'to believe and confess the doctrine of salvation, taught and delivered by the Prophets and Apostles is an infallible and inseparable note of the true Church of God.'[134] He further argued that the doctrine of the Church of England agreed with the early church, 'for the ground and foundation of religion, our churches agree with the churches after Christ, which continued for the space of six hundred years, for we do not only allow of the Apostles' Creed, but of the four general counsels, and of their confessions and creeds.'[135] Thus he asserted: 'For we hold, believe, and maintain, and preach the true faith, that is, the ancient doctrine of

---

[131] Perkins, 'An Exposition of the Creed,' in *Works*, 5:383. An asservation is a solemn assertion or declaration.

[132] Perkins, 'An Exposition upon Christ's Sermon in the Mount,' in *Works (1626-31)*, 3:264.

[133] Perkins, 'An Exposition upon Christ's Sermon in the Mount,' in *Works (1626-31)*, 3:62.

[134] Perkins, 'An Exposition upon Christ's Sermon in the Mount,' in *Works (1626-31)*, 3:65; 'An Exposition upon the Epistle of Jude,' in *Works (1626-31)*, 3:503.

[135] Perkins, 'An Exposition upon Christ's Sermon in the Mount,' in *Works (1626-31)*, 3:62.

salvation by Christ, taught and published by the Prophets and Apostles as the book of the articles of faith agreed to in open Parliament do fully shew.'[136] He also believed that 'our English confession ... the Articles of Religion established in the Church of England' contained 'the foundations of the Christian religion, allowed and held by all evangelical churches.'[137] Nor was the Church of England's adherence to evangelical doctrine merely a matter of words. Perkins argued that 'our church is ready to maintain and confirm the same doctrine by the shedding of their blood.'[138] In view of all this, Perkins stated that 'there is just cause our Church should be reputed the true Church of God, and a good member of his Catholic Church.'[139]

Perkins also defended the worship of the Church of England, a matter of significant dispute in Elizabethan England. He considered the statement, 'It may be said that the Church of the Protestants observes Holy Days.'[140] He noted that, 'Some churches do not: because the Church in the Apostles' days had no holy day, besides the Lord's day: and the fourth commandment enjoins the labour of six days.'[141] In contrast to this strictness, Perkins noted that:

> The Church of England observeth holy days, but the Popish superstition is cut off. For we are not bound in conscience to the observation of these days: neither do we place holiness or worship in them: but we keep them only

---

[136] Perkins, 'An Exposition of the Creede,' in *Works (1626-31)*, 1:307.

[137] Perkins, 'An Exposition upon Christ's Sermon in the Mount,' in *Works (1626-31)*, 3:65.

[138] Perkins, 'An Exposition upon Christ's Sermon in the Mount,' in *Works (1626-31)*, 3:65. Perkins gives the example of England's stand against Spain. Perkins, 'An Exposition of the Creed,' in *Works*, 5:383.

[139] Perkins, 'An Exposition upon Christ's Sermon in the Mount,' in *Works (1626-31)*, 3:65. Perkins would go so far as to say of the Church of England that she was 'our beloved Mother'. Perkins, 'An Exhortation to Repentance,' in *Works (1626-31)*, 3:409.

[140] Perkins, 'A Commentaries upon the Epistle to the Galatians,' in *Works (1626-31)*, 2:286 [titled p288 in the printing, but this is an error].

[141] Perkins, 'A Commentaries upon the Epistle to the Galatians,' in *Works (1626-31)*, 2:286.

for order's sake, that men may come to the church to hear God's word. And though we retain the names of Saints days, yet we give no worship to Saints but to God alone.[142]

He notes that in other areas, such as images, the Church of England had advanced beyond the worship of Rome, 'And therefore commendable is the practice of the Church of England, that suffers not in places that serve for the use of religion, images either painted or carved, no not ... [even] the history of the Bible painted.'[143] Again it is therefore correct to conclude that 'Perkins affirmed and took satisfaction in the doctrinal standards of the Church and ... found its government and liturgy theologically acceptable.'[144]

Even if it was argued that the government and worship of the Church of England was not as it should be—for example, that it should be aligned more closely with Genevan ideals—Perkins held that was no grounds for separation.[145] Those who argued the Church of England 'to be no church because it maintaineth not that outward order they think should be in it' were mistaken, because even if these were errors, they do not touch the 'foundation' of what makes a true church. The true church, as has been seen, is known by 'preaching of the word, administration of the sacraments ... and the use or the power of the keys in admonitions, suspensions, excommunications.'[146] As no one disputed these marks,

---

[142] Perkins, 'A Commentaries upon the Epistle to the Galatians,' in *Works (1626-31)*, 2:286. See also the statement that 'Although we retain the names of saints days in the Church of England, yet are we altogether free from the idolatry; because we dedicate the days themselves to the honour of God.' Perkins, 'The Idolatrie of the Last Times,' in *Works (1626-31)*, 1:683.

[143] Perkins, 'The Idolatrie of the Last Times,' in *Works (1626-31)*, 1:685. Perkins here is arguing that "the painting of the history of the Bible, though otherwise lawful in itself, is not expedient in Churches: because danger of idolatry may arise thence."

[144] Patterson, *William Perkins*, 51. Perkins also stated plainly that the Church of England was one where idolatry was "condemned to the pit of hell". (Perkins, 'The Idolatrie of the Last Times,' in *Works (1622-31)*, 1:670.)

[145] He acknowledged that 'there is controversy among us touching the point of ecclesiastical regiment'. Perkins, 'An Exposition of the Creed,' in *Works*, 5:383.

[146] Perkins, 'An Exposition of the Creed,' in *Works*, 5:384.

'the difference between us is only touching the persons and the manner of putting this government in execution. And therefore men on both parts ... remain brethren and true members of the church.'[147] Thus, with regard to the government of the Church of England, 'though we may prefer church before church, yet we must not condemn a church to be no church for some corruptions that be therein: a true brother may have some blemishes, and a true church some wants.'[148]

But while Perkins was a defender of the established church, he acknowledged that it was a mixed church.[149] He bewailed, 'Alas, how may thousand we have in our church, who know no more in religion than they hear in the common talk of all men ... and which is worst of all, whereas they might have more, they will not, but care not for it.'[150] Perkins was deeply conscious that there were two sorts of individuals in the church: 'And so it is with God's church at this day; in it there be two sorts of men; one, which baptized and brought up in the Church, hear the Word, and receive the sacraments; but yet are not saved ... The other sort are they, which being baptized in the Church, hear the Word effectually, and

---

[147] Perkins, 'An Exposition of the Creed,' in *Works*, 5:384.

[148] Perkins, 'Exposition upon the First Three Chapters of Revelation,' in *Works (1626-31)*, 3:329. Thus, Perkins felt that if the distinction between foundation and secondary truths were maintained 'many which have separated themselves from the Church of England, had still remained members of it.' Perkins, 'An Exposition upon the Epistle of Jude,' in *Works (1626-31)*, 3:585.

[149] This was, by definition, true of every visible church, for 'in visible churches are two sorts of men: just men and hypocrites'. Perkins, 'An Exposition upon the Epistle of Jude,' in *Works (1626-31)*, 3:504. See also, Perkins, 'An Exposition of the Creed,' in *Works*, 5:377.

[150] Perkins, 'An Exhortation to Repentance,' in *Works (1626-31)*, 3:421. See also, Perkins, 'Exposition upon the First Three Chapters of Revelation,' in *Works*, 4:597-8, 600-602. This is not to say Perkins felt the Church of England lacked the power of discipline. Indeed, the reverse, as Perkins argued that 'Which power of the keys in opening and shutting heaven by the ministry of the word, seeing we have established by the Lawes of the land, we have the state of a true church, and therefore no man can in good conscience separate from us.' Perkins, 'An Exposition upon the Epistle of Jude,' in *Works (1626-31)*, 3:503. However, he was conscious it was not always used as it should be. Perkins, 'Exposition upon the First Three Chapters of Revelation,' in *Works*, 4:420.

receive the Lord's Supper worthily.'[151] Because 'the elect are mingled with the wicked in the same assemblies', this meant that the preacher had to aim for conversions, 'therefore the Ministers of the Gospel ought indifferently to exhort all and every one to repent.'[152]

Thus, while criticising those who separated from the Church of England, Perkins still acknowledged its failures:

> For us in England, the case undoubtedly standeth thus: Our Church is doubtless is God's cornfield, and we are the corn-heap of God: and those Brownists and Sectaries are blind and besotted who cannot see that the Church of England is a goodly heap of God's corn: but that withal we must confess, we are full of chaff; that is, of prophane and wicked Hypocrites ... many of our best professors ... do give themselves too much liberty in too many sins.[153]

Indeed, Perkins lamented the spiritual condition of the English church. He said, 'the body of our people seem to be alive by their outward profession, but indeed they are dead in respect of the power of godliness ... men content themselves with an outward profession, but the spiritual

---

[151] Perkins, 'A Commentarie upon the Eleventh Chapter to the Hebrews,' in *Works (1622-31)*, 3:118. Perkins held that 'sacraments are ... for the elect only.' (Spinks, *Two Faces of Elizabethan Anglican Theology*, 67.) Thus, he could say, 'The reprobate, though God offer the whole Sacrament unto them, yet they receive the signs alone without the things signified by the signs: because the sign without the right use thereof, is not a Sacrament to the receiver of it.' (Perkins, 'The Order of the Caused of Salvation and Damnation' in *Works (1622-31)*, 1:72.) For a general study of Perkins on the sacraments, see Spinks, *Two Faces of Elizabethan Anglican Theology*, 69-92.
[152] Perkins, 'A Treatise of Predestination,' in *Works (1622-31)*, 2:608.
[153] Perkins, 'An Exhortation to Repentance,' in *Works (1626-31)*, 3:425. He could even say, 'we are a people of Sodom, as full of iniquities as they were.' Perkins, 'An Exhortation to Repentance,' in *Works (1626-31)*, 3:422. Brownists and Sectaries are designation for followers of the separatist Robert Browne (1550s – 1633).

life of grace is not to be seen.'[154] He felt that 'a great part of the body of our Church hath left off their first love, and the greatest part hath no love at all.'[155] Using a powerful image, Perkins held that 'Our nation is dark and blind in the in the sun-shine of the gospel.'[156] He complained of a prevailing 'general state of ignorance.'[157] Yet, while the Church of England had its faults, 'yet this many be said in behalf of our church, that the wants thereof are not such as do in any way raise the foundation of Religion, or of God's holy worship, and so cannot make it cease to be a true church, and therefore none ought to separate from it for such wants.'[158] This strong affirmation of the Church of England was not to preclude the possibility of further reformation in the church, indeed, 'God's servants may in godly manner desire the Reformation of things that be amiss: for a good church may be bettered.'[159]

To further defend its status, Perkins compared the Church of England with Jerusalem of Jesus' day. Jerusalem then, 'was a true church of God' despite being 'very corrupt both for doctrine and manners as Christ's severe reproof[s] of both doth plainly shew.'[160] Nonetheless, despite its

---

[154] Perkins, 'Exposition upon the First Three Chapters of Revelation,' in *Works (1626-31)*, 3:329. Perkins was clear that 'this doth not prejudice the state of our Church to nullify it from being the church of God'. Perkins, 'Exposition upon the First Three Chapters of Revelation,' in *Works (1626-31)*, 3:329.

[155] Perkins, 'Exposition upon the First Three Chapters of Revelation,' in *Works (1626-31)*, 3:269.

[156] Perkins, 'An Exhortation to Repentance,' in *Works (1626-31)*, 3:420.

[157] Perkins, 'An Exhortation to Repentance,' in *Works (1626-31)*, 3:424. See also, Perkins, 'Exposition upon the First Three Chapters of Revelation,' in *Works*, 4:514-5.

[158] Perkins, 'An Exposition upon Christ's Sermon in the Mount,' in *Works (1626-31)*, 3:65. Thus the church 'repel[ed] the heresies of popery, Anabaptists, and Family of Love and suppress all doctrines which raze the foundation.' However, it tolerated many who 'by deed and conversation deny Christ Jesus.' Perkins, 'Exposition upon the First Three Chapters of Revelation,' in *Works*, 4:482.

[159] Perkins, 'An Exposition upon Christ's Sermon in the Mount,' in *Works (1626-31)*, 3:65.

[160] Perkins, 'The Combat Between Christ and the Devil,' in *Works (1626-31)*, 3:388.

faults, the status of Jerusalem in Jesus' day as a church shows clearly that none should reject the Church of England. As Perkins states:

> though our sins and abuses be many and grievous, yet ... as our Saviour Christ and his disciples joined themselves to the to the congregation of Jews in their legal service and forsook them not till they became no church: so it ought to be among us, till we separate from Christ, none should sever themselves from our church, ministry, and service of God.'[161]

For Perkins, to leave the Church of England because of its failings was therefore 'far from the spirit of Christ, and his Apostles.'[162] Indeed Perkins bemoaned 'the rigour and austerity of many in too severe censoring of offenders and offences', arguing that this is 'the sin ... of those that are departed from our church condemning us (for some wants) utterly as no church.'[163]

In view of all this, it is correct to say that 'Perkins ... considered the established Church sound in its liturgy, polity, and doctrinal standards, though he saw it hampered by inadequate teaching and preaching.'[164] And that 'His [Perkins'] vocation was thus not so much to alter the established Church of his time as to make it more effective and its teachings better known and appreciated.'[165] Therefore, notwithstanding his acknowledgements of its faults, Perkins was proud of the Church of England, 'Look at the outward face of our church, at the signs of God's love which are amongst us, and at God's dealings with us; and behold,

---

[161] Perkins, 'The Combat Between Christ and the Devil,' in *Works (1626-31)*, 3:389.

[162] Perkins, 'The Combat Between Christ and the Devil,' in *Works (1626-31)*, 3:389. Perkins was aware that his arguments could potentially be used to decry the Protestant separation from Rome. But Perkins placed Rome in a different category, as will be discussed below. For example, see Perkins, 'The Combat Between Christ and the Devil,' in *Works (1626-31)*, 3:389.

[163] Perkins, 'An Exposition upon the Epistle of Jude,' in *Works (1626-31)*, 3:587.

[164] Patterson, *William Perkins*, 62.

[165] Patterson, *William Perkins*, 63.

we are a most beautiful Church, a glorious Nation.'[166] Thus it is right to say: 'He has no sympathy with the advocate of separation over questions of church order; as long as the Church was committed to Reformation Orthodoxy and he himself free to teach, preach, and apply that orthodoxy, his Anglican loyalty would not be in doubt, even when he had to endure harassment from within the system ... loyalty to the established system was integral to the Christianity he taught.'[167]

The Church of Rome

If that was Perkins' view of the Church of England, what then of Rome? Is she a true visible church? The answer is 'yes and no', or perhaps better, 'no and yes.' Perkins was insistent that:

> If by this church be understood a state of regiment of the people, whereof the Pope is head, and the members are all such as do acknowledge him to be their head, and do believe the doctrine established in the Council of Trent; we take it to be no Church of God.[168]

However, matters are not that simple. The Church of Rome is clearly in a different category to what Perkins calls 'congregations of Turks and

---

[166] Perkins, 'An Exhortation to Repentance,' in *Works (1626-31)*, 3:422. This needs to be tempered by Perkins' frank acknowledgment that 'the state of our church continuing as it is, nothing can be expected but judgements from the Lord.' This judgment was not due to the form of government or doctrine of the church, but the laxity of many of its members. Perkins called all in the church individually and corporately to repent. Perkins, 'Exposition upon the First Three Chapters of Revelation,' in *Works*, 4:494. See also Perkins, 'Exposition upon the First Three Chapters of Revelation,' in *Works*, 4:602; 621.
[167] Packer, *An Anglican to Remember*, 17-18.
[168] Perkins, 'A Reformed Catholike,' in *Works (1626-31)*, 1:617. See also, Perkins, 'A Commentarie upon the Eleventh Chapter to the Hebrews,' in *Works (1626-31)*, 3:167; 'Exposition upon the First Three Chapters of Revelation,' in *Works (1626-31)*, 3:342; 'An Exposition upon the Epistle of Jude,' in *Works (1626-31)*, 3:514; 'An Exposition of the Creed,' in *Works*, 5:380.

other infidels.'[169] Why is that? In Islam, 'there is no means to salvation at all' but with Rome 'the true church of God is and hath been in the present Church of Rome, as corn in the heap of chaff.'[170] This state of affairs exists because Rome has the 'means to salvation ... the Scriptures, though in a strange language: and baptism, for the outward form.'[171] The baptism of Rome was, as such, to be regarded as valid baptism, because 'there is in the Church of Rome, the hidden Church of God.'[172] Still, because Rome was in a state of 'universal apostasy' God's people were not to join in her communion for God 'will not have them for external society to be mixed with their enemies.'[173] Rather than being the 'spouse of Christ', Rome is 'spiritual Babylon, the mother of abominations ... a strumper.'[174] Indeed, Perkins argued that 'there is no more concord between these two religions [Protestantism and Rome], than between light and darkness.'[175] How can he say this when, ostensibly, they hold 'the same Word, the same

---

[169] Perkins, 'A Reformed Catholike,' in *Works (1626-31)*, 1:616. See also, Perkins, 'An Exposition of the Creed,' in *Works*, 5:380; 'Exposition upon the First Three Chapters of Revelation,' in *Works*, 4:536.

[170] Perkins, 'A Reformed Catholike,' in *Works (1626-31)*, 1:616.

[171] Perkins, 'A Reformed Catholike,' in *Works (1626-31)*, 1:616. Perkins was clear that 'baptism in the Church of Rome is severed from true faith, or from the Apostolic doctrine: and the outward baptism is severed from the inward baptism. For they of that Church overturn justification by the mere mercy of God, which is the principal part of inward baptism.' Perkins, 'A Commentaries upon the Epistle to the Galatians,' in *Works (1626-31)*, 2:256. For further comment, see Perkins, 'An Exposition upon Christ's Sermon in the Mount,' in *Works (1626-31)*, 3:17.

[172] Perkins, 'Cases of Conscience,' in *Works (1626-31)*, 2:73. See also, Perkins, 'A Commentaries upon the Epistle to the Galatians,' in *Works (1626-31)*, 2:256; 'Exposition upon the First Three Chapters of Revelation,' in *Works (1626-31)*, 3:329; 'An Exposition of the Creed,' in *Works*, 5:381; 'Exposition upon the First Three Chapters of Revelation,' in *Works*, 4:545-6.

[173] Perkins, 'A Reformed Catholike,' in *Works (1626-31)*, 1:616-7.

[174] Perkins, 'The Combat Between Christ and the Devil,' in *Works (1626-31)*, 3:389.

[175] Perkins, 'An Exposition upon Christ's Sermon in the Mount,' in *Works (1626-31)*, 3:17. Rome 'in truth and before God is dead.' Perkins, 'Exposition upon the First Three Chapters of Revelation,' in *Works*, 4:545.

Creed, the same Sacraments?'[176] He believed that 'they do quite overturn the foundation of the Bible, the Creed and of the Sacraments: as in the points of justification by works, of human satisfaction, of worshipping saints and images, and their massing sacrifice and priesthood may soon appear.'[177] Rome quite simply 'doth not bring her children to seek God' and 'teaches not her children to seek God in the right way.'[178] Those who are saved within the communion of Rome are saved in spite of her, not because of her. Yet, through her continued use of the sacrament of baptism, the Apostles' Creed and scripture, 'God hath there his secret church, who never yielded to the Pope's government and doctrine.'[179] However, at the end of the day, for Perkins, Rome 'is a rotten and dead corpse void of spiritual life. And therefore we have separated ourselves from the Church of Rome upon just cause; neither are we schismatic in so doing, but they rather, because the ground and proper cause of schism is in them.'[180]

---

[176] Perkins, 'An Exposition upon Christ's Sermon in the Mount,' in *Works (1626-31)*, 3:17.

[177] Perkins, 'An Exposition upon Christ's Sermon in the Mount,' in *Works (1626-31)*, 3:17. See also, Perkins, 'An Exposition of the Creed,' in *Works*, 5:380-1; 'The Combat Between Christ and the Devil,' in *Works (1626-31)*, 3:389. In the latter reference, Perkins argues that Rome lacks succession with apostolic doctrine, that baptism alone is an insufficient mark of a true church and that Rome in her doctrine and practice utterly vitiates the teaching of the Creed and of scripture.

[178] Perkins, 'A Commentarie upon the Eleventh Chapter to the Hebrews,' in *Works (1626-31)*, 3:32.

[179] Perkins, 'Exposition upon the First Three Chapters of Revelation,' in *Works (1626-31)*, 3:329.

[180] Perkins, 'An Exposition of the Creed,' in *Works*, 5:382. Rome, among other things denied that the 'kingdom of Christ was spiritual and not of this world' in seeking to govern with 'the civil sword' as well as 'the sword of the word' showing 'Rome is from hell, not from heaven'. Perkins, 'Exposition upon the First Three Chapters of Revelation,' in *Works*, 4:498. See also, Perkins, 'Exposition upon the First Three Chapters of Revelation,' in *Works*, 4:567.

How far can a church fall and remain a church?

But if Rome is really no church, considered in all that makes her distinctive, how far can a church fall and remain a church?[181] Perkins considers that question in his commentary on Galatians. He notes that 'the Galatians had made a revolt, and were fallen from justification by the obedience of Christ ... and yet he called them churches still.'[182] Perkins argued that we must follow Paul's example 'in giving judgement of the churches of our time.'[183] He gave three rules to enable judgment to be given on whether a church is still worthy of that title. They should be familiar by now. First, Perkins is insistent that 'if the faults of the church be in manners, and these faults appear in the both in the lives of ministers and people, so long as true religion is taught, it is a church.'[184] Perkins' point here is that the bad living of people or ministers does not give grounds for separation from a church.[185] Nevertheless, on a personal basis, it is permissible to 'separate from the company of bad men in the church ... and, if it be in our liberty and choice, join to churches better ordered.'[186] That is, it is permissible to attend the services of a sounder local congregation if that is an option, as it might be in a large city.[187]

---

[181] As well as Rome, Perkins said 'Libertines, and Anabaptists, and family of Love ... they are no churches of God, for they hold against the foundation.' Perkins, 'Exposition upon the First Three Chapters of Revelation,' in *Works (1626-31)*, 3:286. See also, Perkins, 'An Exposition upon the Epistle of Jude,' in *Works (1626-31)*, 3:585.

[182] Perkins, 'Commentary on Galatians,' in *Works*, 2:19.

[183] Perkins, 'Commentary on Galatians,' in *Works*, 2:19.

[184] Perkins, 'Commentary on Galatians,' in *Works*, 2:19.

[185] See also, Perkins, 'An Exposition upon Christ's Sermon in the Mount,' in *Works (1626-31)*, 3:66-67. Perkins held that it 'may be said of them who preach wholesome doctrine, though their lives be still offensive ... in doctrine they be with Christ and must so far be approved.' Perkins, 'An Exposition upon Christ's Sermon in the Mount,' in *Works (1626-31)*, 3:241.

[186] Perkins, 'Commentary on Galatians,' in *Works*, 2:19.

[187] Perkins is not advocating founding differing denominations of 'true' churches. Such a concept would be utterly alien to his thought.

However, if the error is doctrinal rather than practical, the next rule is to 'consider whether a church errs in the foundation, or no.'[188] If the error is not in the 'foundation of religion' then 'Paul has given the sentence that they which build on the foundation [with the] hay and stubble of erroneous opinions may be saved (1 Corinthians 3:15).'[189] A church may therefore have many doctrinal errors before it is permissible to separate from it. Example errors which do not affect foundational truths are 'when a Lutheran shall hold that images are still to be retained in the church, that there is a universal election of all men, etc. For these and such like opinions may be maintained, [with] the foundation of salvation unrazed.'[190] By contrast, foundational truths are 'the denial of the death of Christ and the immortality of the soul, justification by works, and the like ... the sum of these fundamental points is comprised in the Creed of the Apostles and the Decalogue.'[191]

Perkins' third rule was that 'inquiry must be made whether the church err of human frailty, or of obstinacy.'[192] Perkins' view here is that it is possible for a church to err, even in the fundamentals, and still be a church—as long as that error is still correctable. However, 'if a church shall err in the foundation openly and obstinately, it separates from Christ, and ceases to be a church, and we may separate from it and may give judgement that it is no church.'[193] The churches of Galatia had 'erred

---

[188] Perkins, 'Commentary on Galatians,' in *Works*, 2:19. See also, Perkins, 'An Exposition of the Creed,' in *Works*, 5:372.

[189] Perkins, 'Commentary on Galatians,' in *Works*, 2:19.

[190] Perkins, 'An Exposition of the Creed,' in *Works*, 5:379. Perkins was very clear that Lutheran churches are 'true churches of God'. Perkins, 'An Exposition of the Creed,' in *Works*, 5:382-83.

[191] Perkins, 'An Exposition of the Creed,' in *Works*, 5:379. For Perkins' outline of how Rome 'disannuls' the Ten Commandments, see Perkins, 'Exposition upon the First Three Chapters of Revelation,' in *Works*, 4:484.

[192] Perkins, 'Commentary on Galatians,' in *Works*, 2:19. See also, Perkins, 'An Exposition of the Creed,' in *Works*, 5:379-80.

[193] Perkins, 'Commentary on Galatians,' in *Works*, 2:19. The example Perkins gives is Paul's separation from the Jewish church owning to its final and ultimate rejection of apostolic teaching regarding Jesus Christ. See also, Perkins, 'Exposition upon the First Three Chapters of Revelation,' in *Works (1626-31)*, 3:286.

in the foundation' but 'Paul had now only begun in this epistle to admonish with the Church of Galatia.'[194] As such, before any church is left, even where foundational truths are compromised, significant time must be given for remedying the error. A further example is the church of Sardis, described in Revelation 3 as 'dead.' Yet Perkins notes that 'this was a true church of God', despite being 'in a very corrupt state, both in regard of outward conversation, and of sundry erroneous opinions.'[195]

When should we leave a church?

It is almost impossible to overstate Perkins' reticence to separate from a church. He looked to the practice of Jesus himself. He noted that the 'church of the Jews' in Jesus' day was 'exceedingly corrupt.'[196] The corruptions that Perkins pointed out included: 'the office and place of the high priest was bought and sold' and 'the Scribes and Pharisees, which were doctors of that church, erred in some fundamental points of doctrine, teaching justification be works.'[197] And yet, for all this, 'Christ did not separate from that church, nor teach his disciples so to do.'[198] Perhaps even more astonishingly he argued:

> When the Jews had crucified the Lord of Life they remained a church ... the Apostles acknowledged that the covenant and the promises still belonged unto them: and they never made any separation from their Synagogues, till such time as they had become sufficiently convicted by the Apostolical ministry that Christ was the true Messiah.[199]

---

[194] Perkins, 'Commentary on Galatians,' in *Works*, 2:19.
[195] Perkins, 'Exposition upon the First Three Chapters of Revelation,' in *Works (1626-31)*, 3:329.
[196] Perkins, 'An Exposition upon Christ's Sermon in the Mount,' in *Works (1626-31)*, 3:65.
[197] Perkins, 'An Exposition upon Christ's Sermon in the Mount,' in *Works (1626-31)*, 3:65.
[198] Perkins, 'An Exposition upon Christ's Sermon in the Mount,' in *Works (1626-31)*, 3:65.
[199] Perkins, 'An Exposition of the Creede,' in *Works (1626-31)*, 1:307.

Even those who were guilty of crucifying the Lord Jesus, even they did not immediately cease to be a church. But Perkins did believe that separation from a church in certain circumstances was legitimate, after all he was not still in the Church of Rome! He explicitly considered the question: 'at what time a man may with good conscience make separation from a church?'[200] He answered first in the negative, that is: 'So long as a church makes no separation from Christ, we must make no separation from it.'[201] But by contrast, 'when it separates from Christ, we may also separate from it.'[202]

But how can it be known when a church separates from Christ? Perkins outlines two ways of knowing this.

> The one is, where the worship of God is corrupt in substance ... When Jeroboam has set up idols in Israel, then the Priests and Levites came to Judah and Jerusalem to serve the Lord. The second is when the doctrine of religion is corrupt in substance ... A practice of this we have in the Apostle Paul, who being in Ephesus in a Synagogue of the Jews, spake boldly for the space of three months ... but when certain men were hardened and disobeyed, speaking evil of the way of God, he departed from them and separated from the disciples at Ephesus [from them as well, Acts 19:9].[203]

These are high standards, the literal worshipping of golden calves and the literal rejection of the gospel for another religion (Judaism). Perkins made two further points. He reiterated his common refrain that sinful living of those in the church was no grounds for separation, 'As for the corruptions that be in the manners of men that be of the church, they are no sufficient warrant of separation, unless it be from private company.' [204] For example, the presence of unworthy recipients of the sacraments did

---

[200] Perkins, 'An Exposition of the Creede,' in *Works (1626-31)*, 1:307.
[201] Perkins, 'An Exposition of the Creede,' in *Works (1626-31)*, 1:307.
[202] Perkins, 'An Exposition of the Creede,' in *Works (1626-31)*, 1:307.
[203] Perkins, 'An Exposition of the Creede,' in *Works (1626-31)*, 1:307.
[204] Perkins, 'An Exposition of the Creede,' in *Works (1626-31)*, 1:307.

not damage the sacrament for believers, as 'another man's evil conscience cannot defile thy good conscience ... Christ ... communicated with the wicked Jews.'[205] And, in this context, he again made the point that separation from the Church of England was unwarranted, and indeed sinful, 'By this which hath been said, it appears that the practice of such as make separation from us, is very bad and schismatical, considering our churches fail not either in the substance of doctrine, or in the substance of the true worship of God.'[206] Patterson's summary is therefore correct: 'regarding separation from the Church, Perkins recognized only two circumstances in which a course of action would be justified—namely, if the worship of God were corrupt in substance or if the doctrines of religion were corrupt in substance.'[207]

Why was it such a serious thing to separate from a true visible church? It was serious because, as the Westminster Confession would later say, 'outside of [the visible church] there is no ordinary possibility of salvation.'[208] Perkins himself said that 'we must remember that shut out of the Church there is no salvation.'[209] By this, he meant that 'none can be saved ordinarily from condemnation, that are out of the Church, for in the Church is God's covenant of grace, with the sacraments and the seals thereof.'[210] As such, 'every man must be admonished evermore to join himself to some particular church, being a sound member of the catholic church.'[211]

---

[205] Perkins, 'An Exposition upon Christ's Sermon in the Mount,' in *Works (1626-31)*, 3:67. See also, Perkins, 'Exposition upon the First Three Chapters of Revelation,' in *Works*, 4:420.
[206] Perkins, 'An Exposition of the Creede,' in *Works (1626-31)*, 1:307.
[207] Patterson, *William Perkins*, 51.
[208] Westminster Confession 25:2 in *Westminster Confession*, 107.
[209] Perkins, 'An Exposition upon Christ's Sermon in the Mount,' in *Works (1626-31)*, 3:66. See also, Perkins, 'An Exposition of the Creed,' in *Works*, 5:372.
[210] Perkins, 'An Exposition upon Christ's Sermon in the Mount,' in *Works (1626-31)*, 3:66. See also, Perkins, 'A Commentarie upon the Eleventh Chapter to the Hebrews,' in *Works (1626-31)*, 3:49. Perkins also cites the dictum 'he cannot have God for his Father which has not the church for his mother.' Perkins, 'An Exposition of the Creed,' in *Works*, 5:323.
[211] Perkins, 'An Exposition of the Creed,' in *Works*, 5:372.

Conclusion

What shall we say to these things? What does Perkins' doctrine of the church, his defence of the Church of England and his radical opposition to separation from it mean for us today?

It means many things, but principally this it calls us to have a much higher view of the unity of the visible church than we do. It calls us to have a much higher threshold than we do before we consider leaving a church or a denomination. On a personal basis, Christians move churches for all kinds of reasons: better provision for children, an aesthetic of worship that is more to our taste, a different philosophy of ministry or vision. Perkins would not, and could not, comprehend such a thought process. If the word is preached in accordance with apostolic doctrine, if the sacraments are dispensed and if there is church discipline we have no grounds to leave a church.

There is also a corporate dimension. My own ecclesiastical connections have always been outside the national church, both in Scotland and England. However, I am deeply conscious that the fortunes of evangelicals in the national church do so much to determine the spiritual climate of the nation. As such it has been a deep grief to watch the fragmenting of evangelical witness, as evangelicals have responded so differently to the challenges of the day and so often done their own thing. Ministers leaving one by one, congregations dividing. In an imperfect world, that is perhaps inevitable, but it is nonetheless deeply sad.

We live in a world when the church is drifting further and further from its moorings, in an age when the distance between apostolic teaching and the teaching of the established churches is becoming wider and wider. Realistically, differing responses and judgments are hard to avoid.[212] But I think Perkins calls us to a better way, a united way, perhaps even a

---

[212] For Perkins' strong rejection of ordained women's ministry, see Perkins, 'Exposition upon the First Three Chapters of Revelation,' in *Works*, 4:515-18. By contrast, Perkins strongly defended, understandable in the context of his day, the right of women to 'publicly govern in the commonwealth.' Perkins, 'Exposition upon the First Three Chapters of Revelation,' in *Works*, 4:517.

way shown by the recent unity of conservative Anglican Evangelicals in the Church Society. Perkins undoubtedly raises the bar on when a church ceases to be a church of Christ. He calls us to stay where we are for much longer than our natural inclination might be. Perkins calls us to stay and labour for recovery.[213] But above all, I think he calls us to act together. There may come a time when our national churches cease, in any sense, to be true churches of Christ. That day may be near or far, and surely our prayer is that day never comes. But, if we act together, then the witness of evangelicals will emerge stronger—whatever happens on the larger scene. If we act as individuals, we will find ourselves on our own. Perkins' high view of the visible church and its unity, calls us to stand together—and (may the day never come) to fall together if necessary.

---

[213] This is important. To stay and drift with the prevailing theological climate when the 'foundations' are being attacked is not the apostolic spirit. Perkins calls on churches to 'show forth zeal in excommunicating and casting out such heretics as by damnable doctrine did trouble them.' Perkins, 'Exposition upon the First Three Chapters of Revelation,' in *Works*, 4:481.

If you have enjoyed this book, you might like to consider:

- supporting the work of the Latimer Trust
- reading more of our publications
- recommending them to others

See www.latimertrust.org for more information.

Lex Orandi, Lex Credendi by Martin Davie

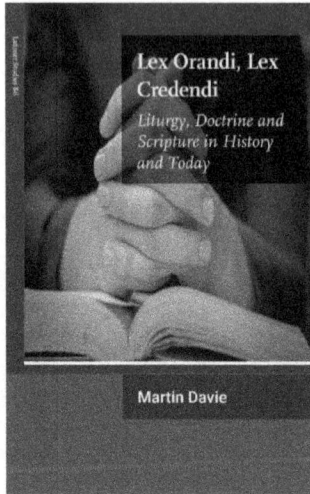

The Latin phrase lex orandi, lex credendi ('the law of praying is the law of believing') is a phrase which is often used in Anglican theological discussion, but which needs careful unpacking if its meaning is to be properly understood.

In this study Martin Davie provides such unpacking. He traces the history of the phrase back to its origin, and gives examples of how it has been both used and misused in the Roman Catholic, Orthodox and Anglican traditions.

His conclusion is that when it is rightly understood the principle lex orandi, lex credendi provides a useful tool for assessing both a church's liturgy and its doctrine. It reminds us that a church's liturgical practice needs to cohere with its doctrine and both need to be in line with Scripture.

And the Light Shineth in Darkness by Kirsten Birkett

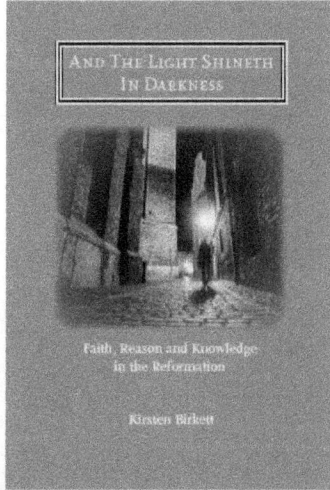

The Bible describes a fallen world and fallen humanity, in which minds are darkened. We reject God, and suppress the truth about him. How, then, can we know him at all? In other words, what are the noetic effects of sin? During the Reformation, doctrines of total depravity and the effects of the fall on the whole person re-emerged, with consequent implications for epistemology. If minds are fallen, how can we expect to know anything accurately? The purpose of this study is to start to answer that question by looking at some of the epistemology we find emerging from the writings of John Calvin and Martin Luther.

Portrait of a Prophet by Martyn Cowan

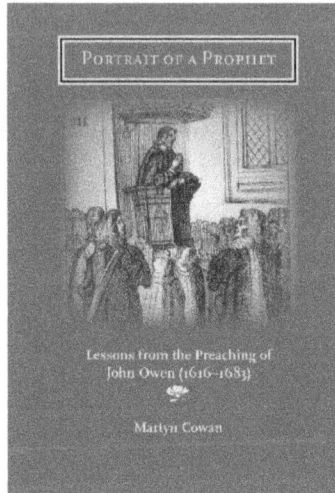

This study offers a sketch of John Owen's prophetic preaching in which his dogmatic providentialism and the fiery apocalypticism almost threaten to destroy his image as a Reformed Orthodox theologian and man of the Renaissance. With an initial glance, one might think that there is little practical to be learned from such a vignette. However, upon closer inspection three striking applications, or, in the language of early-modern homiletics, 'uses', emerge that are directly relevant for much contemporary preaching.

www.ingramcontent.com/pod-product-compliance
Lightning Source LLC
Chambersburg PA
CBHW020441030426
42337CB00014B/1341